20 May 2003

Steve
Thank for
being you
Always Roy

 W9-ATE-268

Vision On Publishing

1

I think the country is a place where people should not choose to live. There is to much killing and robbering going on. I really don't like this country, and I cant wait to get out of it.

Shateea
Harris

Years later, Shateea and her brother were shocked by the photo. They didn't remember taking it at all.

2

WANT i thAAk
OF OThe UNiti
Ned StANts

LAUKI LYONS

4

FOREWORD
**BY PAUL FUSCO
MAGNUM PHOTOS**

In 1995 Lauri Lyons grabbed her camera and an American flag and began an odyssey to discover and reveal the faces and voices of the unknown: Americans who did not bask in the seats of power, who did not control the destinies of mega-corporations, and who rarely appear in news stories. Lauri walked the streets of New York, the bayous and sugarcane fields of Louisiana, the Native American reservations of Montana and everywhere in between. During her journey she found jewels in the faces, hearts, and souls of many Americans and proudly presents them to us.

Lauri's Americans reveal themselves to us through their pride, openness and honesty. They proudly display the banner of America with their hope or stomp it beneath a heavy boot. Given the opportunity to speak their truth without restrictions, they present themselves with a directness and honesty that brings them to life. There is a beauty and power in the stand they all take and Lauri brings her subjects to us with a new insight, depth and great vitality.

Flag: An American Story is a grand journey that opens our eyes and hearts to the inesti-mable value of each human being and the truths that hold our society together; the foundations and promises of America that live in our Constitution and Bill of Rights. Flag is a remarkable achievement.

With a seemingly disarming simplicity and directness Lauri Lyons has taken us on a lyrical and insightful journey into America. Lauri left with her camera and banner and returned with the heart of America securely wrapped in the American flag.

Opposite page: One of Lauri Lyons' four note books, in which her subjects wrote their comments and sometimes criticisms of America.

I love america

Heriberto Cruz

I was shooting at a sugar
cane refinery when Herbrito
approached me. I thought he
was coming to throw me out.
'Do you want me to show
you the factory?'
Nice surprise.

FLAG
an American Story

BY LAURI LYONS

INTRODUCTION
BY LAURI LYONS

What is America?

Beautiful, violent, principled, racist, hopeful, chaotic, always changing. It's such a challenge to try to define this country. America completely re-invents itself on a daily basis. As I set out cross-country to photograph people with the American flag, I wasn't sure what I would find.

Growing up I have been lucky enough to view America from several perspectives: black, female, first-generation American, a former military child. My parents were born and raised in Jamaica, arrived in New York in the 1960s and later joined the Air Force in the 70s. As a family we have traveled the world many times over, putting my opinions, prejudices and outlook on life in constant flux. Always being on the move, and a bit left of center, has made me curious about how people come to formulate solid opinions about themselves and others.

As a college student during the Gulf War, it quickly became apparent to me how little my peers knew about the military's activities or the symbolic power of the American flag. This realization, coupled with the political polls and sound-bytes defining the current American psyche, made me question the validity of the people's opinions that the media represented as fact.

Back in New York, I decided to find out what people really thought about America, keeping the process simple and to the point, without injecting my own beliefs into the outcome. Traveling by subway through the city, I chose neighborhoods I didn't know, and only photographed strangers. I never expected to get anyone to cooperate, assuming most people would think I was a weirdo or an idiot. I was very pleasantly surprised that most of the people I met were really excited and thoughtful.

Brooklyn, Queens, Manhattan and the Bronx. Although they're some of the most exciting, unpredictable locations in America, I became weary of shooting in an urban environment. It felt like every photograph incorporated concrete, a wall,or a panorama of store fronts. I needed a change of scenery, not only to broaden the visual palette but also to reignite my curiosity.

I had an idea of what this country looked like geographically, but wasn't sure whether my assumptions were based on myth or reality. I decided to travel by train so I would be able to see the country, as opposed to flying over it. That decision made a world of difference. The following week I purchased an Ameripass rail ticket from Amtrack and packed a few changes of clothes, a camera, a bag of film and my Rough Guide tour book, and departed on a train from Manhattan en route to Montana.

Within an hour of leaving Manhattan I began to see rolling hills, the rushing Hudson River, farm houses... nature! I was entranced and seduced by the idea of embarking on a great journey, a life-changing experience. Traveling was not

a new experience (having been raised by two military parents), but this was different. This was not an order imposed by the government with a set destination and calculated outcome. This experience would be like America itself: a constant improvisation.

Once I left New York and relaxed into the beautiful scenery passing by, a feeling of fear began to slowly grow inside me. It was not a fear of homicidal maniacs, the Klu Klux Klan or any of the usual things that could endanger a journey: more frighteningly, I was in the middle of a once-in-a-lifetime opportunity, finishing a project I had been working on for years. This was it. The moment had arrived. I was traveling to totally unfamiliar parts of the country, hoping to appeal to people I'd never met, and convince them to take pause in their lives and give the world a piece of their mind. (And I had to find lodging and transportation, learn my way around each new town, get tons of great photos and meet my publishing deadline!)

Traveling by train was a beautiful experience. This was my first trip by rail in the US, and I was pleasantly surprised by how comfortable it was. I was instantly mesmerized by the view, unsure which way to look, because I didn't want to miss anything! En route to Montana, I witnessed the beauty of the vast autumnal farmlands of Indiana and the mounting snow of the Great Lake states. North Dakota had never made my list of exotic destinations, but I was truly blown away by its beauty – the expanses of land, riverbeds, and miles and miles of

sunflower fields. Men drove tractors through golden fields that looked like Shredded Wheat. My first view of Montana was a buffalo amid mountains of haystacks. This was insane: the Hollywood myth was real? I was certain these had to be backdrops.

Glacier, Montana was unbelievably beautiful and cold; that type of cold that immediately closes your pores when you step outside. In order to meet as many people as possible, I walked up and down every street in town. Word quickly spread that a crazy girl was walking around trying to photograph people. I was also the only black person in town. Everyone knew who I was! Everyone in Glacier was exceptionally friendly and genuinely interested in making the project a success. Without their help, Glacier would have been impossible to shoot. I was there during the off season when tourists leave and the town reverts back to the few locals. They fed me and drove me through their town, the national park and Canada. They also let me photograph them and their friends. Truly great people. In Montana I learned about buffalo burgers, huckleberry pie, branding cattle, and life on the range and the reservation: nature, history and politics all under one big sky.

Now that I was into a rhythm of shooting, my original fears began to ease. Instead, during those frequent nights when I had nothing to do, thoughts of homicidal maniacs did cross my mind a couple of times... I think I saw every late-night TNT and USA Network movie ever made. I was always thankful when the sun rose. On the average day, I woke up around 7 AM, checked the weather forecast, went out for breakfast, made a game plan of where I should shoot, began shooting by 10 AM and ended shortly before dusk. Usually after dinner I would be spent and retreat to my bed. If I had gone out at night, I would have been an item of interest to the locals, and have to explain why I was in town. It was too much work after walking around and shooting for seven straight hours.

After leaving Montana, I was on to the great Northwest. The geography changed from immense fields and sky to dense forest and moisture. The train wound through woodland that looked as if it was being discovered for the first time. Fog hovered above the soaring trees and down below in the basins.

Next I hit Seattle: the new cyber frontier with progressive politics, Starbucks and Nirvana. It was that and a whole lot more. I immediately located the nearest youth hostel and claimed a drafty room with a funky futon mattress and dirty communal bathroom. I began shooting immediately after checking in – and instantly realized that there are two Seattles. The first is a well-planned, efficient city which boasts comfortable hippies, hard-working new immigrants and, of course, young cyber-people sending emails on their laptops while drinking a dizzying array of coffees. The other Seattle doesn't show you what it's got until the sun goes down! Drugstore cowboys, runaways, panhandlers, skate punks, goths and musicians... and they're

all white! New York has the same cast of characters, but they're a much more diverse crowd. Seattle was unexpected, changing so dramatically within a few hours. The night crowd seemed particularly young... not trendy thirty-year-olds, but white middle-class teenagers. If mainstream news and magazines are to be believed, the only people down and out and going through social angst are blacks and Latinos. Reports in the media are always romanticized. Seattle unexpectedly illustrated the gap between the empowered and the disillusioned.

As soon as I left, it rained in Seattle for five days straight. I had made it out just in time, and began my odyssey down the mythical West Coast en route to San Francisco. From the lush Oregon country-side to the radiant Pacific Ocean: logging, cliffs, sailboats and old docks. I was definitely excited about going to San Francisco. One of the oldest cities in the US, it is fabled for earthquakes, gold, immigrants and a rarely matched zest for life. I was pleased to see that it lived up to its reputation. Within an hour of arriving, I settled into a youth hostel, and on a search for food, I was asked by a woman on the street if I was a hooker! I was sorry to disappoint her, but very amused – I must have looked really good or really crazy! Either way, anything that got people to come up to me and make conversation was all good.

Photographing in San Francisco was amazing. Everyone was so open and up for anything. I loved the drifter who used my cell phone to call his family in Oregon, the missionaries who paged me to set up a time to be photographed, Charity the pregnant girl from Philadelphia and so many others. I would also like to thank all the homeless people who helped me navigate through the city and watched my back. Without them I would have been lost, knowing my terrible sense of direction. After postponing my departure ticket several times I finally had to peel myself away from that alluring city.

In order to leave San Francisco I boarded a bus to southern California, making my way to the Los Angeles Union Rail Station. From there I caught a train to New Iberia, Louisiana, definitely the longest route of the journey. The sun-baked red clay dirt of Arizona and the pastel mountainous land of New Mexico were accented by cactus, rainbows and spectacular lightning storms. And then there was Texas. Texas is big, real big! I thought it would never end and the train would just fall off the edge into the abyss... with small towns, pick-up trucks, cotton fields and the Rio Grande. A major wake-up call is those few feet of water that separate El Paso from Mexico. To the left stand skyscrapers and to the right lies poverty.

Louisiana is exactly what I thought it would be: green, swampy and overgrown. And after a long haul through dry, flat west Texas, I was very happy to see it. Anyone who takes more than three minutes to get off the train will miss the New Iberia stop – the town is that tiny. There I met Sarah Moss, who let me stay at her house and drove me into town

every day. In New Iberia I was re-acquainted with small-town Southern hospitality: real white picket fences, RV vans, homecoming parades, gumbo and a little-known delicacy called "fried baked potatoes". I was also aware of the South's eerie past and present. Old slave cabins are now converted into sheds, mixing with Confederate Army graves and newly built plantation-style houses. The people in the South are much more relaxed about who they are and how they think they will be perceived. It also helps that no one seems to be in a great rush to get anywhere, so it was quite easy to approach people. But, boy, was it hot! My sweat was sweating.

From New Iberia, I quickly passed through New Orleans and pushed further north to Memphis, Tennessee, hoping to get to Nashville before the rain hit. By the time I arrived in Memphis, after so many weeks of shooting all day and starting over every morning, I was out of my mind with travel delirium. All of the habits I had followed so meticulously, such as basic safety, budgeting and time management, flew by the wayside. I wanted to get the hell out of Dodge and go home. I was exhausted. The night I arrived in Memphis, the first youth hostel I passed looked more like a haunted house, with tomb-stones in the yard and all! It scared the shit out of the taxi driver and me, and we immediately made a u-turn. I decided on a cheap motel. While inside registering, I waved to the driver to wait for me. A few seconds later I turned around and discovered no cab, no driver, no bags, nothing – he thought I had waved good-

bye! Luckily he came back with my luggage, but it was definitely time to go home. I ate some barbecue, saw one of the most unique wonders of the world, Graceland, and broke out.

Miami was great. Hot, but not sweat-on-top-of-sweat hot. Miami is a better version of LA: a beautiful landscape (that you can see), and a diverse mix of people (who actually venture out of their cars and walk on the streets)! I expected to find a carnival-type atmosphere, and I did: bathing beauties, political activists, cross-dressers and street prophets. The final afternoon of the trip I met Slim Shady, the last person I photographed for this book. He was wearing Mickey Mouse boxers, white pumps and the American flag. With a deep Southern accent he told me he was from Paris, asked me for a kiss and gave me the peace sign. In a strange way he embodies all of the cultural contradictions of being American. As Americans we are who we choose to be, and that may all change tommorow.

Lauri Lyons

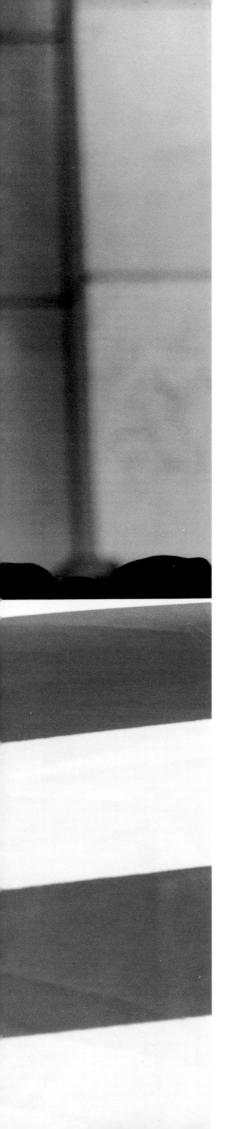

I THINK That This Contery is way below STandards WE HAVE TO becume AS ONE before WE All FAIl APARt From Each other.

VERONICA KEYS

Veronica waiting for the bus in Minneapolis. Only enough time for one exposure.

By WILL, THE U.SA is a good place to LiVE, but there can be Up's and down's, LiKE POOR housing, bad jobs that don't pay Nothing even good job's that don't pay nothing IF there can be A chang towards jobs, Housing, eCONOMics systen and bad Schooling and the way iNdividual think. The world would BE A better place to live

by Will Robinson

Will was just back in town and trying to reacquaint himself with his family.

what I think about the country. I don't
like it because to much killing and crime.

SEELA Ramdial

LOVE is MY MISSION IN LIFE.

John McLoughlin

THE MIDDLE CLASS IS A THING OF THE PAST THE ONLY PEOPLE THAT CAN SURVIVE ARE THE RICH & THE POOR. THE MIDDLE CLASS WORKS FOR THE RICH & PAYS TAXES, WHICH ARE HIGHER & HIGHER EVERY YEAR TO SUPPORT THE POOR.

BERRY RISPOLI '88

Berry fixes Harleys and lives for Harleys in Brooklyn.

We like American because it is beautiful and we are also free

Monique Jackson   Joise Barlow   Keisha Vander

After each frame the little girls would scream at the top of their lungs for the boy to keep still. Finally he gave up, got bored and rested on the Madonna.

U.S.A. — I all should answer the call
to freedom. we are only slaves to our
own minds. Love is always the way!
God bless

Jane McMillian

Looking for peace it's not far
away just look inside of your
heart and soul.

Dennis S. McMillian

A couple from Michigan
visiting Miami. They knew
something was up because
I kept staring at them with
the 'photographer stare'.

What I THINK about AMERICA / well to make a long story SHORT, I must say AMERICA has treated me well but I took Advantage of the FREEdom other people don't get the chance to have. I'M AN EX-gang member that fell INTO THE life of drugs and crime I did alot of prison time most of my teenage and the best years of my life behind a wall and IN a fucking cell that made me feel as if I were some kind of fucking animal. But now I'm slowly getting my shit together to better my life in the ghetto. I'M a fARther and a mother to my 8 year old son. And that's why now in time I'm a different person and I'm always going to be a fuckiNS different person cause to tell you the truth in this WORLD IF you don't help yourself and do → right thing you aRE fucking history. THANK you for letting me Right about the way I really fucking feel about AMERICA.

SAMMY
F.M.D
FILthy
MADDOGS MC.

Sammy from Park Slope
took my instructions to
'be brutally honest' very
seriously.

Amos 9:8
AMERICA WILL BE Destroyed
By Jesus CHRIST AND THE
ANGELLIC FORCES

Gen 25:25
THEIR TRUE NAME OR BIBICAL
NAME IS THE EDOMITES THE
CHILDREN OF ESAU

John 8:44
THE So-CALLED WHITE MAN
IS THE DEVIL THAT THE
BIBLE SPEAKS OF.

JERE 14:2
THE REAL JEWS ARE THE So-CALLED
NEGROES. GOD, JESUS CHRIST, THE Angel.
THE Israelites = children of GOD are
                BLACK

A NYC Isrealite in full effect
in Times Square.

I Like the city Because PeopleareNice. I DontLike The city
BeCausePeople are suting other people.

Alisa Conyers

A sweet little girl just leaving
Catholic school in the Bronx.

ELDER KATA & I (ELDER IRISH) ARE MISSIONARIES FOR THE CHURCH OF JESUS CHRIST OF LATTER DAY SAINTS. WE FEEL
EXTREMELY BLESSED TO LIVE IN A COUNTRY WHERE "WE CAN CLAIM THE PRIVILEGE OF WORSHIPING ALMIGHTY GOD
ACCORDING TO THE DICTATES OF OUR OWN CONSCIENCE, AND ALLOW ALL MEN THE SAME PRIVILEGE, LET THEM WORSHIP
HOW WHERE, OR WHAT THEY MAY." (11 ARTICLE OF FAITH) I THINK AS CITIZENS OF THE UNITED STATES WE HAVE A
TENDENCY TO TAKE OUR BASIC RIGHTS FOR GRANTED. HOW TRULY BLESSED WE ARE!

*Elder ... ...
Elder ... Kata*

Young Mormons who
needed permission from
their leader to participate
in the project. I was sure
I would never hear from
them again. They later
paged me with permission
granted.

Coming from cold, conservative London, Miami is sunny, free + relaxing + New York has a wonderful trendy buzz. So I think America is great, and I'll definately be back!

Lynn Van Vark

I chased this woman for what felt like a half a mile down the beach. She reminded me of a Miami Ursula Andress.

BASICALLY AMERICA IS THE LAND OF OPPORTUNITY BUT YOU HAVE TO REALLY
GO ALL OUT FOR WHAT YOU BELIEVE IN. I LOVE AMERICA BUT IT STILL
NEEDS ALOT OF IMPROVEME IN THE EQUAL OPPORTUNITY AREA.

Michael Baker

Iv Trauile a lot this
is the best in this Country

Lennis J. Romero

I love my Country
and the people are nice
in St. martinville

Ophe J Romero

The Romero brothers, the
most famous citizens of St
Martinville. They sit out all
day and sing Cajun songs
in French.

My thoughts of America. America has got to be
the greatest Country in the World. It provides
freedom of Speech as well As freedom To do And
Go Any where one Wishes Too. It is just
Great To be An American.

Berword Mitchell, JR

The Deputy Sheriff. I saw
him having breakfast in the
morning. I also found him
later that evening: 'I thought
you forgot about me.'

Jonathan CARROLL
Jonathan Carroll

JAMES. CHERRY
James Cherry

There were originally three
men sitting down. As soon
as I pulled out the flag the
middle man got up and
said, 'I'm not being photographed with that flag'.
Easter Sunday, Harlem.

America is a shithole the government is completely fucked up, unrepresentative of the people, and ever creeping towards a total dictatorship. Beware

America,
I love my country (hate the politics 2000!)
Great people, wonderful place
Every region is different New Orleans Texas
Washington N.Y.C., San Antonio, Key West
Miami

Sandra Damicone

Sandra the engineer was definitely on holiday and feeling good: 'Now girl, you know my legs are spread wide open!'

No MORE DRUGS, NO MORE race troubles, better family life,
no more Killings of children. More Love in the world.
People need Jesus

Marty

THIS IS ONE OF THE RICHES COUNTRY BUT ONE
OF THE DUMMIES. THEY RATHER HELP OTHER THEN
THEIR OWN.
          SLEEPY

Hi My Name is Guy Clark they Call me the Flower Man and God Bless America

Guy Clark

The flower man who has been selling flowers on the same corner for twenty years. 'I want to wear the flag as a sarong with my African hat, holding my flowers.'

I Think most Americans Have lost Touch with Musical Culture. In most other Countries Traditional Music Part of Life, Here its just A Pop Culture And people Dont Realize or Respect where it Came from. If its Not A Hit people Dont Want to Hear it.

Hobie Ginnis

The bartender in San Francisco who knows every song that was ever made.

I think that the us is unfair
because they don't give a dam about
all the black people that live in
this world. by shanta
A.K.A
Kool-Aid

I think the United States is a backwards
Country because they busy trying to help
other countrys instead of helping their selves.
Lakeya

I think this country needs to work alot on helping homeless. Noone should have to sleep on the street unless they choose to. Noone should starve

Charity Holley

Charity usually sits in this spot. As soon as I started photographing her, people began to give her money and the guy in the store next door came out and gave her some food.

The ultimate paradox of good living
on the backs of all others

Michael
Dobee

USA WAS R U OK
Cowboy Ray

America, like stepping stones that tumble, some fall with the flow, some utilize the growth. And there is the MAN for everything to point the finger at, And each of us are him.

Huneefah

I'm A FOLK (YEAH LYRICAL) SONGWRITER AND I'm STUMPED WITH THIS
QUESTION OF AMERICA LET US LOVE US ALL AND BY GOD TAKE
RESPONSIBILITY FOR OUR-SELVES WITHOUT EXPECTATION FROM OTHERS
THANKS—

Katy
KATYKLAIRE

Katy was doing her thing in
the park and gearing up for
a gig later that night.

I like this country Because theres mad Bitches mad Herbs and Hs Just great Jonathon Guzman

I think this country is messed up This country needs alot of Things changed But we know that will never happen. Jenny Rosentho

Everyone's favorite couple.
Jonathan was just chillin'.

America you have many treasures and
the most valuable of them are your people.
Please don't throw them away.

VALENCIA HAWKINS

I Dont like this world because there is so much madness and people that love to fight. I hate the police and the stupid things they do throwing people against the wall and shit. I would like to live in a nice world with out all the crimes and people that love to fight

Christina Tarantino

Christina's homeless friend
begged her to take the
picture. 'I ain't holdin' that
flag. Throw it on the ground.'

I like America because there are very
nice people who cares for us one thing
I like America too is because there
are things to do and people to meet.
                                        Damarie Esguerra

They were so excited to be
photographed, and rounded
up more of the family for
the photo.

GEOGRAPHICLY: BEAUTIFUL
CULTURALLY: BLAND
POLITICLY: FUCKED
POLITICAL PRISONERS IN
THE LAND OF THE FREE
UNCONSCIOUSNESS IN THE
INFORMATION AGE.
CORPORATIONS RULE THE
GOVERNMENT OF THE PEOPLE...
THINGS HAVE GOTTA CHANGE.

Stefani

THE BASIC NOTIONS THAT AMERIKKKA
IS BASED ON — FREEDOM FOR ALL,
EQUAL OPPORTUNITY, JUSTICE FOR
ALL — IS ALL LIES. THIS IS ONE
OF THE MOST UN-COMPASSIONATE,
INHUMAIN, REPRESSIVE SOCIETY'S OF
ALL TIME. AND ANYONE WHO SAYS
OTHERWISE IS EITHER UNINFORMED OR
PROFITING FROM IT.
WAKE UP!   STAND UP!
FIGHT FOR YOUR RIGHTS BEFORE
ITS TOO LATE!
— ARROW →

East Village squatters with a
lot on their mind.

57

I like New york becuse I make
a lot of friend and becuse it's fun!

Danielle and cathy

I think that this country should change
because of a lot of violence.

Delroy Baxter   Sade Blanfaud   Abdullah Blanford

The Country is a Place that is nice and
calm. I also love to Rodeo and rope and
ride on the ranch. That is what I
like about the country.
                    Colt and Colyn Doce

The U.S. Is a good place to live.
Very beautiful especially the county
I live in, Glacier country, MT.

                    Tyrel Smith

Rancher kids helping to
brand 700 head of cattle.
I knew I was really out there
when I climbed into a cow
pen to take a picture.

I Think the United States
Is good. It has to Be
BECAUSE everyone
wANts to come here.
Fran Cimato

To me I'm glad I
was boRn iN The U.S.
MARie AnnaRumo

I LOVE THIS COUNTRY

Richard Misrach

'I knew you wanted to take a picture of me. I could tell by the way you looked at me.'

I think the oil country is great.
As long as the work keeps coming

Tommy Trahan
John.H. Oliver

'Hey, what you doing?
Taking pictures?
Take a picture of me and
my friend.'

I THINK America is a Great Place to live but I think it Needs many Changes. For One the government needs to look for people in need here and see that the people are using there funds as what there are given for. There are alot of children in hungry here that they need to see and take action of. I Also feel the president need to tax people just like they do for Social Security One lump sum and finish with that. That way every one would pay same Amount as all. As for Child support I feel both parents should be responsible for the child and pay same amount. not put only one parent responsible for child both should play a part in that which means they both are responsible and not one. Just because one parent keeps the Child doesn't mean she or he should collect from only one that's one thing that should be considered. I feel parents are using there childs money for themselves and not for children.

Diane Carlson
LisA T Williams

I have mixed feelings about the country I live in. Sometimes I love living here and somtimes I dont. I dont like the man definition of beuty all of our modlles look unhealthu. But on the other hand we have very good schools, and justice system But I think our country is pretty darn cod in the long run.

Emma H.

'Oh no! You're gonna take a picture of us? But we've got all this junk!'

Being a teenage minority in San Francisco, in America makes you think twice about
where you go. Every place you enter you have to think about what you are getting into you
have to be carefull because there a lot of people out there and there has to be someone
who can harm you.

There are many things wrong in America — but there are many things wrong in the world — At least there are no bombs falling around us — no tanks rumbling down our streets. So perhaps we may be able to right some of the wrongs. As long as peace exists there is a possibility for positive change. I LOVE AMERICA !

Sarah Moss

Sarah Moss: the craziest woman in Louisiana.

IT is nice I Like

Amber Lee Romero

I Love American Country

Mary Jane Leleux

'Can you take a picture of
me with my Senior Olympics
medal?'
What did you win it for?
'Shuffleboard. And I'm good
at throwing horse-shoes too!'

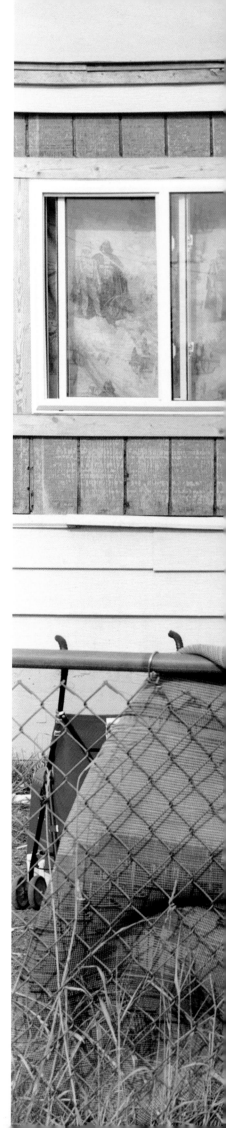

My Name is Kenny Little Dog I'm from, Browning Montana on the Blackfeet reservation. I'm a Full-Blood Blackfeet Indian. Some things I don't like around here is the discrimination in Montana between Indians and whites. What goes on here is Jealousy and hatred as well between us Blackfeet Indians. too bad we all can't get along with one another.

A. I. M.

Kenny Little Dog

Kenny Little Dog. The first person I photographed on my road trip.

The country is good. The neighborhood
is bad. Cause there is to much drugs enwolved.

andrew

My name is Anthony Richards I came to this country in the year of 1983. I felt like It was the greatest thing that I ever did Because this is the land of many people And I feel that is country is good in many way.

Anthony Richards

this country is the Best.
I Like going outside everyDay
NABiL

LIVING IN THE USA MEANS FREEDOM TO ME & MY FAMILY!
TO BE ABLE TO SPEAK & TO THINK FREELY IS A VERY
PRECIOUS RIGHT!

'I'm an old hippie, and I love
to go outside with my coffee
and just say hello to people.
They look at me like I'm
crazy.'

Montana, "Spoken of in Hushed and reverent tones"! Truly a life worth
living Montana Indian, Cowboy Country, and loving it!

HILSON

I THINK THAT THIS COUNTRY IS AII
HATE AND IS FUII WITH TOO MUCH
CRIME VIOIACE
                    JAY F.T.
                    BROWN.

I THINK THAT THIS COUNTRY IS
TO SAD AND TO HATEFUII.
                    PAPPA
                    RAN. PT

THANKS TO OUR VETERANS AMERICA
IS #1

James V Castrogiovanni

I Think America is a
Great Country To Live in.
~~Both~~ But The Government
Is more Comunist Then Cuba.
The Government Needs to Start
Taking Care Of its own
People, Than worring about
Taking Care of people ~~over~~ in
Other Countries. ~~Th~~ I think
The Government Needs To Take
Care of Americas problems
First Before worring about whats
Going on else~~where~~where Then
America Would be A better Place.

About Racism and sexuality.
Me myself being a homosexual
male in this Country. You Get →

alot of hate from other
People. That Make you Feel
Worthless. Maybe one day
This Country Would straighten
Up. All The Violence ʒ Racism
ʒ Hate needs To Stop. So we
can all live in a better World.

John Breaux

What America means
to me. It means my Right
to Say what i want. The
freedom to reach out to
other people. I really Love
America.

Denise Robertson

American is 2 beautiful
Place to live; but
people who are haters
and evil make it bad.
Ruthie Hill

Great country, with a lot of oportunitis for foreign people
like me. this country remenber me when my GRAND FATHER
told me about our country in the past (ARGENTINA) that necibe
with open Arms people all from All world to give new
oportunitis. thank usa

Santiago Urrea

I feel that america is so good it has good people, and beautiful women that is very dazzling. America has a beautiful sun set. It has lots of jobs for many people of all kinds even homeless-people. I met a beautiful black girl her name is Juri. America has good beaches for people to have fun in the sun. Hi my name is, Slim Shady and I am a Gods gift to women. *Love you*

The last person I photographed for the book. I was on my way back to my room when I met 'Slim Shady'. Where are you from? 'Darlin', I'm from Paris, France,' he said with a Southern twang.

I AM A PROUD GUARDIAN Angel. I AM A SOUTH AFRICAN & AMERICA WAS A NEW EXPERIENCE FOR ME. I HAD FUN, LOADS OF OPPORTUNITIES ONLY THING MOST OF THE PEOPLE ARE EXTREMELY RUDE The CHEWING GUM WAS THE MOST DISGUSTING THING OF ALL AMERICA is TRULY A LAND OF OPPORTUNITY

Angel's

I moved to the USA when I was 15 years old. I like it. Very different than a third world country. I joined the Guardian Angels, and I have enjoyed it I joined to learn Self-defense because I didn't want anyone to harm me physically.

Anna K Sahadeo

WHEN ASKED to VOICE MY OPINION ON AMERICA & Society All I CAN SAY is ONE VOICE, ONE PERSON MAY NOT MAKE A DIFFERENCE, But if THAT VOICE CAN ECHO, it's A GOOD START That's why I'm A GUARDIAN ANGEL TODAY!!

KRICKITT

.is a German Irish American —
I find America the pits —
it is a fake facade of
Justice and Democracy.

I FIND THAT LIFE IS EASY.
BECAUSE YOU make it EASY

A national health care plan is the largest unmet need in America today. We are demanding that our government provide health care for all Americans, regardless of their inability to pay. Access to gene therapy should be part of this care.

Jennifer Johnson
Londa Summers
Joyce Y. Lindeman
Diane Harvey
Pat Schwarz

Women on the move. When I saw them turn the corner I thought 'This can't be real!' After taking their photo I heard one woman say, 'Wait 'til I tell George!'

I think that that this country is the best state you
could live in and I predict that people from other state's
should move here.

Bianca
Hernandz

I'd like the country from fridom in it

I think that this place we live is bad cause to many people are bad and killing I wish that Bayridge would be a nice place to live *Veronica Acosta*

'What are you girls doing out there?'
'Taking a picture.'
The aunt then moved towards the window with the baby.

United States Is The best Country in the World.
I am Colombian, been here fourteen years, but the
freedom I have here, speech, movement, religion
nothing and no other country compares. Also,
My daughter Is American.

Daniel Martinez

I had to take his picture.
He was perfect.
Talk about relaxed!

Things I think about the country is that it's being run very wrong and People should stand up and do something about it.

Tyrell Jones

Tyrell was perfect
mid-sentence.

THE U.S IS THE GREAT COUNTRY, I LIKE YOUR PEOPLE AND YOUR FOOD. THIS COUNTRY IS BEAUTIFUL, AND FREEDOM. I LOVE AMERICA.

Andrea Morano.

The moment every family knows: beach chaos.

LAND OF THE THIEF, HOME OF THE SLAVE (MENTALY OR PHYSICALLY) YOU CLAIM THERE'S PEACE
BUT I'M LABELED A BEAST. IT's NOT JUSTIFIED FOR 1 MAN TO KILL ANOTHER BUT IN THE
OTHER HAND IT's JUSTIFIED TO STARVE, WHICH LEADS TO DEATH HUNDREDS OF PEOPLE IN CUBA
WITH YOUR SANCTIONS? RED: IS FOR THE BLOOD THAT THEY SHED FOR THE WHITE: SUPREMACY ALL OVER
THE SEVEN SEAS! LOVE PEACE AND MULTIP
                                        BLESSINGS
DAVE CLARKE
     TITO

Tito was about to burst with
excitement. 'I've been
waiting for something like
this to happen all my life!'
When he smiled he had a
mouth full of braces. He
was only 15.

WHAT I Think about AMERICA?

'Its Beautiful if you allow It to be, theres Different Routes you Can take In america Positive and Negative I WAS once positive but I Fell victim To the Negative respect of Life Do to the Fact that Im A victim of Drugs. But now my mind & Body IS About to change. I will get Life together where As It can help bring Society back In time My Goal IS to Be a Drug Counselor And I will Seek It very Fast, I WANT So Bad to Help our younger Brothers & Sister. Because they will be the Ones to Make America a better place to Live. One Love

Danny Dee MaGic

Danny Dee. On the road back to recovery.

105

AMERICA IS A COUNTRY <u>WITHOUT</u> A SOUL: "LAND OF THE FREE; HOME OF THE BRAVE" - ??!!
IT HAS BEEN A TREMENDOUS DISAPPOINTMENT TO ME, ESPECIALLY RE-THE MYTH OF "AMERICA, THE BEAUTIFUL"
THAT HAS BEEN EXPORTED WORLD-WIDE, ESP. TO 3RD WORLD COUNTRIES. YOU SEE, WE <u>BELIEVED</u> IT. BUT IT IS A
DELUSION, A TRAGIC DISTORTION & MISREPRESENTATION OF THE TRUTH. MAYBE ONCE, AMERICA WAS A SHADOW OF
THE DREAM IT PERPETUATES, BUT <u>NOT</u> NOW. NOW THE GOD IN AMERICA IS MONEY, THE ALMIGHTY $. AMERICA FOR ME,
ISN'T REAL, ITS <u>FAKE</u> - IN EVERY WAY. THE LIFESTYLE IS PSEUDO, THE SMILES ARE PSEUDO, THINGS ARE NOT AS
THEY APPEAR, & THERE IS A GREAT AURA OF DECEPTION ABOUT EVERYTHING. BUT THE BIGGEST THING IS THE PEOPLE:
THEY RELATE TO YOU ON AN ENTIRELY SUPERFICIAL, <u>OUTER</u> LEVEL. AMERICANS HAVE LOST TOUCH WITH THEIR BASIC
HUMANITY AS A WHOLE. AMERICANS NEED TO GET BACK TO THE BASICS UPON WHICH THIS GREAT LAND WAS
FOUNDED, BACK TO THEIR GOD AND THEREFORE BACK TO "<u>LIFE</u>, <u>LIBERTY</u>, AND THE PURSUIT OF HAPPINESS."

Deborah Hughes.

Deborah from Trinidad.
'What the hell are these
people trying to say ?!'

No One Can Choose your own mountain for
you or tell you how to climb

Rev. J Bellinger

I think America needs a big improvement on the environment, simply because there's lots of people throwing out trash in front of other people's houses and won't think twice of what problems they've caused.

Riva Barras

In this great land of opportunity, follow your goals even when you may fail, keep trying and you will succeed!

Alfred Bolognini

Marie Bolognini

Two snowbirds from New Jersey, who won a trip to Miami through work.

I Dont like America Becaus of the Cursing, mugging,
voilence and all those Homeless i relly feel Sorry
for those people i hope they get a home But if you
go Visit people in the Different States they are real
nice and the places are Beautiful to. Huma Sheikh
Naila Chawdry

I have Lived in this place all my life. America is the greatest place around, But in some places I Turn and Look around and I see poverty. But the government doesn't really give a damn about it.

Like the great 2-pac shakur Said "They have money for guns and war but can't fad the poor". Now the other thing I want to talk about is racism. "Never judge a book by its cover". but all I see is people being judged by the color of their skin. We need to get over this racial hump and come together as one.

What I have written please give It thought, Because this is something thats earned not ever bought.

Timothy (T-boy) Carlson

'I was in love once, but it must've had a big ol' trampoline down in there, cause I bounced right on out!'

Dear Society
as the brother smooth tacl June Bot and Sham sterlin keeps
it real and feel that the society should try no to degrade us for
every mistake we make and we dont mean no harm but if thing
were better we would be better But if thing dont get better soon
Brother who cant cope will start

flip the script on who ever get up there and when they
get there aint no turning Back Baby the goverment that
locks us up wont give us Jobs strait up Baby!
                    PEACE
        am   June   eddie
        sterlin   Bot   Burguss

All of them were really into
taking the photo. When I
was finished I realised none
of them knew each other.
The guy with the fur asked,
'How did you ever notice
me?!'

This Cant tree sucks the big We We!

Jon boy

Three drifters on the West Coast. After taking the photos my cell phone rang. Later the guy in the middle said, 'I want to ask you a favour. Can I use your phone to call my family in Oregon?' They had not heard from him in a year.

I fell great to be an american

Emmett Charles

The sweetest security guard.
He had to be 80.

The Land of the FREE!
and home of the BRAVE!!
what else do I need to say.

Ryan Conway

Ryan, who drove me all over
Glacier and into Canada.